The TEN COMMANDMENTS

By REV. LAWRENCE G. LOVASIK, S.V.D.
Divine Word Missionary

CATHOLIC BOOK PUBLISHING CO.
NEW YORK, N. Y.

Dear Boys and Girls:

GOD made you for heaven. He wants you to be happy with Him in heaven because He loves you with a love that has no end. To go to heaven you must not only know God, but you must love and obey Him. Jesus said, "If you love Me, keep My Commandments." Jesus teaches you how to do all this through the Catholic Church.

If you love Jesus, you must keep the Commandments of God and of the Church.

This book will tell you what these Commandments are. Ask Jesus to help you to obey them, just as He always did what His Father wanted Him to do.

Your friend in Jesus and Mary,

Fr. Lawrence S.V.D.

GOD MADE ALL THINGS

GOD made the world and all the good things in it. God made me.

God made me to show His goodness and to make me happy with Him in heaven. To be happy with God in heaven, I must know Him, love Him, and serve Him in this world.

I love and serve God by keeping His Commandments.

"Look how beautiful the stars are. They always do what God wants them to do."

THE TEN COMMANDMENTS

ALL the laws of man must be based on the Ten Commandments. They teach me how I must love God and my neighbor as myself.

Mr. Jones shows that he believes in the Ten Commandments when he puts his hand on the Bible and promises to tell the truth in court.

THE TEN COMMANDMENTS

I. "I am the Lord thy God: thou shalt not have strange Gods before me."

II. "Thou shalt not take the name of the Lord thy God in vain."

III. "Remember thou keep holy the Lord's day."

IV. "Honor thy father and thy mother."

V. "Thou shalt not kill."

VI. "Thou shalt not commit adultery."

VII. "Thou shalt not steal."

VIII. "Thou shalt not bear false witness against thy neighbor."

IX. "Thou shalt not covet thy neighbor's wife."

X. "Thou shalt not covet thy neighbor's goods."

Only if I keep God's commandments can I be happy forever in heaven.

God gave Moses His Ten Commandments on Mt. Sinai.

FIRST COMMANDMENT

I MUST love God and pray to Him because He made me – and I owe Him my love.

I sin against FAITH by not believing what God has made known to us, and by taking part in non-Catholic services.

I sin against HOPE when I do not trust God.

I sin against CHARITY when I do not love God and my neighbor; when I am lazy in saying my prayers; when I am jealous of people; when I give a bad example to anyone.

I must offer to God alone the highest worship that He deserves.

I worship God:
by believing in God,
by hoping in God,
by loving God,
by adoring God,
by praying to God.

"Jesus, I love You!" Kathy and Donald always stop at the church to say a prayer.

SECOND COMMANDMENT

"Thou shalt not take the name of the Lord thy God in vain."

I MUST honor the name of God and never say anything that is not nice about God and the saints and holy things.

I take God's name in vain when I use the name of God or the holy name of Jesus without reverence. I will bow my head when I say or hear the holy name of Jesus.

Danny took Mildred's doll, but he says, "Honest to God, I didn't take it!" He is not only taking God's name in vain, but also telling a lie.

I must not curse. When I curse I wish evil upon a person, place, or thing.

I must try never to get angry and curse. Instead, I will say, "Jesus, help me!"

When I hear anyone curse, I will say, "My Jesus, mercy!"

Richard is making fun of Joan because she is reading her prayer book. Instead of getting angry, Joan says a prayer to herself, "Please help me, Jesus!"

THIRD COMMANDMENT

"Remember thou keep holy the Lord's day."

I MUST go to Mass every Sunday and holyday. Holy Mass is the greatest gift I can offer God to adore and thank Him; to ask His pardon and to beg His help.

This family never misses Mass. They are very happy because God blesses them.

We must not do hard work on Sunday. It is a day of prayer and rest. God gives us six days; it is only fair to give Him one day.

Every Sunday I will say some extra prayers at home or read a book that will help me to love God more, or make a visit to church in the afternoon.

Louis is a farm boy. On Sunday afternoon he likes to take a walk in the fields and see the many beautiful things God has made.

FOURTH COMMANDMENT

"Honor thy father and thy mother."

I MUST love, respect, and obey my parents and all who are over me. They take God's place. When I love them, I love God.

As a boy, Jesus helped Saint Joseph with his work in the carpenter shop. He also helped His Mother at home. He gave Mary and Joseph love, respect, and obedience. This made them very happy.

I obey my father and mother when I do at once what they tell me to do. I should try to help them in their work, and never hurt them by anything I do or say.

If I should disobey my parents, or make them angry, I will tell them that I am sorry. I will always try hard to make them happy because I want to be like Jesus.

Mary Ann is helping her mother with the wash, while Larry is helping his father paint.

FIFTH COMMANDMENT

"Thou shalt not kill."

I MUST be kind to everyone, and not quarrel and fight. I should try not to get angry or to get even with my playmates.

I must take care of my health. But, most of all, I must take care of my soul by going to Holy Communion often and also by praying.

The fifth commandment obliges us to take proper care of our body by eating nourishing food.

When I fight I try to hurt others. But God wants me to love everybody, even people I do not think are nice.

I will try never to get angry at anyone, or to get even when anyone has hurt me. I must not lead others into wrong by my words or actions.

I must always give a good example to other boys and girls.

Billy is trying to make Jimmy fight, but Jimmy does not want to; he knows it is wrong.

SIXTH COMMANDMENT

"Thou shalt not commit adultery."

I MUST be pure in all I see and hear, say and do.

I will pray to the Blessed Virgin Mary that she may keep me pure. Every day I will say three Hail Marys and after each Hail Mary these words:

"O Mary, by Your Immaculate Conception make my body pure and my soul holy."

Paul knows it is a sin to do anything impure. He confesses the sin as soon as he can.

I will never speak impure words, or look at bad pictures, or touch myself or anyone else in an impure way.

If I am pure and modest, God and the angels and saints will love me. I cannot be a friend of God and the devil at the same time.

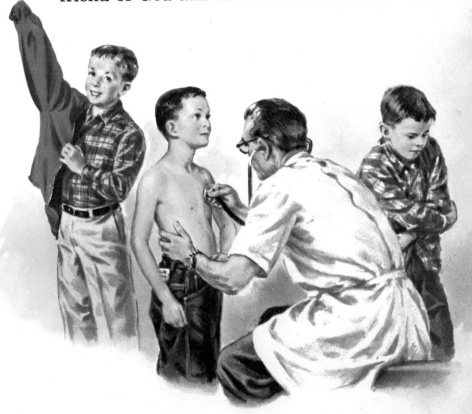

Every boy wants to keep his body healthy and strong. A good boy wants to keep his soul healthy and strong by being pure. Then he will really be following Jesus and Mary.

SEVENTH COMMANDMENT

"Thou shalt not steal."

I MUST not steal or keep what belongs to others.

Jesus said that if God takes care of the birds and flowers, He will take care of me, too. I do not have to steal.

"Don't take that orange, Eddie! That's stealing!"

I must always be honest and fair in all things. It is wrong to cheat.

I must not damage the property of others, or keep what belongs to others.

I must return to the owner anything that has been stolen, or else pay for its value.

The team that plays fair always wins in the eyes of God and people, even if it does not win the game.

EIGHTH COMMANDMENT

"Thou shalt not bear false witness against thy neighbor."

I MUST never harm the name of others by saying unkind things about them.

I will never talk about the faults of others, because I have no right to judge others. Jesus said, "Judge not, and you will not be judged."

These children always pray for their neighbors. They do not talk about them.

I must never tell a lie. I must always be truthful even if I know I shall be punished.

A person who is always truthful is noble and brave. "Honesty is the best policy."

When Johnny hit a car with a stone, he did not run away, but he said to the owner. "I threw the stone, sir, but I am very sorry."

NINTH COMMANDMENT

"Thou shalt not covet thy neighbor's wife."

I MUST be pure in all I think and want. If my thoughts are pure, my actions will also be pure.

Jesus said that only the pure of heart will see God.

When two people are married, they are allowed to think about and do certain things to show their love.

When an impure thought comes to my mind, I will ask Our Lady to help me get rid of it.

In Holy Communion Jesus helps me to be pure in my thoughts and actions.

I will receive Holy Communion as often as I can — at every Mass, if I can — so that the grace of this sacrament may keep me pure in thought and desire.

Your mother and father love each other. They find great happiness in their home and family.

TENTH COMMANDMENT

"Thou shalt not covet thy neighbor's goods."

I MUST be satisfied with what I have, and not want what does not belong to me.

I will try to help those who need my help. Jesus said, "What you do for the least of my brethren, you do to Me."

Jesus wants you to be kind to others, not selfish. Try to share your good things with others, even if they are not your friends.

Jesus said to the rich young man, "Sell what you have and give the money to the poor."

I must not wish to take or keep anything that belongs to another.

It is wrong to envy others because of the good things they have.

I must never be glad that someone else is sad.

Michael got a new bicycle for Christmas and Bobby is sad because his friend is happy.

JESUS said: "If you love Me, keep My commandments."

God is good. If I keep His commandments, He will make me happy on earth and forever in heaven.

This is a happy family because father, mother and children keep the commandments of God and of the Church.

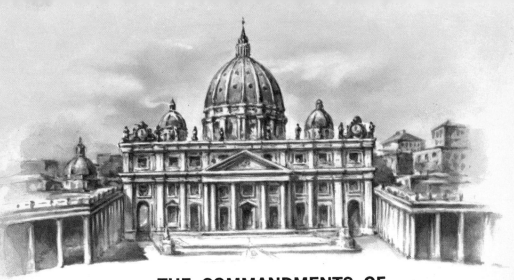

THE COMMANDMENTS OF
THE CHURCH

OUR Lord Jesus Christ gave His Church power not only to teach us what we must believe, but also to command what we must do to save our souls. These are the six chief Laws of the Church:

1. To assist at Mass on all Sundays and holydays of obligation.

2. To fast (take only one full meal) and to abstain (eat no meat) on days appointed.

3. To confess our sins at least once a year.

4. To receive Holy Communion during the Easter time.

5. To c o n t r i b u t e (pay our share) to the support of the Church.

6. To observe the Church's laws concerning marriage.

PRAYER

TEACH me, teach me, dearest Jesus,
    In Your own sweet loving way,
All the lessons of *obedience*
I must practice day by day.

Teach me *meekness*, dearest Jesus,
Of Your Heart the gentlest art;
Not in words and actions only,
But the meekness of the heart.

Teach me generous *love*, dear Jesus,
To make use of every grace,
And to keep Your just Commandments
Till I see You face to face.

Teach *obedience*, dearest Jesus,
Such as was Your daily bread
From the crib of Bethlehem
To the Cross on which You bled.

Teach *Your Heart* to me, dear Jesus,
Is my most important prayer;
For all grace and virtues
Are in richest beauty there.